This publication has been
made possible
by a grant from the
National Endowment for the Humanities
Washington, D. C.

The Chinese Exhibition

A pictorial record of the
Exhibition of Archaeological Finds
of The People's Republic of China

National Gallery of Art
Washington, D.C.
December 13, 1974-March 30, 1975

The Nelson Gallery-Atkins Museum
Kansas City, Missouri
April 20-June 8, 1975

Asian Art Museum of San Francisco
The Avery Brundage Collection
San Francisco, California
June 28-August 28, 1975

TITLE PAGE

Calligraphy by Kuo Mo-jo
Vice-Chairman of the Standing Committee of the
National People's Congress of The People's
Republic of China
President of the Academy of Sciences of China.

The Committee for the Organization of Exhibitions of
Archaeological Finds of The People's Republic of
China has supplied the majority of photographs and
other graphic material appearing in this publication.

Robert Harding Associates, Ltd., London and
The Times Newspaper Ltd., London, have supplied
the remainder.

Cover Photo: Per-Olle Stackman, Stockholm

COVER

218 Bronze Galloping Horse (detail)

FRONTISPIECE

139 Pottery figure of a squatting woman (detail)

PAGES x AND xi

218 - 234 Bronze chariots, horses, and warriors
unearthed at Wuwei (detail)

CONTENTS

THE EXHIBITS

Numerals refer to exhibit numbers

COMMITTEES

THE UNITED STATES COMMITTEE OF HONOR FOR THE EXHIBITION OF ARCHAEOLOGICAL FINDS OF THE PEOPLE'S REPUBLIC OF CHINA

Dr. Ronald Berman
Chairman
National Endowment for the Humanities

Mr. Frank T. Cary
Chairman
International Business Machines Corporation

The Honorable C. Douglas Dillon
President
The Metropolitan Museum of Art

Mr. William E. Goetze
Chairman
Asian Art Commission
San Francisco, California

The Honorable Mike Mansfield
Majority Leader
United States Senate

Mr. Milton McGreevy
Senior University Trustee
The Nelson Gallery-Atkins Museum
Kansas City, Missouri

Mr. Paul Mellon
President
National Gallery of Art, Washington

The Honorable Thomas P. O'Neill
Majority Leader
United States House of Representatives

The Honorable John J. Rhodes
Minority Leader
United States House of Representatives

The Honorable John Richardson, Jr.
Assistant Secretary of State for Educational
and Cultural Affairs

The Honorable Hugh Scott
Minority Leader
United States Senate

Dr. Frank Press
Chairman
Committee on Scholarly Communications with
The People's Republic of China

The Honorable Charles W. Yost
Chairman
National Committee on United States-China
Relations, Inc.

THE COMMITTEE FOR THE ORGANIZATION OF
EXHIBITIONS OF ARCHAEOLOGICAL FINDS OF
THE PEOPLE'S REPUBLIC OF CHINA

Wang Yeh-chiu
Chairman of the Committee
Director of the State
Administrative Bureau of
Museums and Archaeological Data

Hsia Nai
Vice-Chairman of the Committee
Director of the Institute of
Archaeology
Academy of Sciences of China

Wang Chih-fan
Member of the Committee
Permanent Council Member of
Chinese People's Association
for Friendship with Foreign
Countries

Hsiao Teh
Member of the Committee
Deputy Director of the Information
Department,
Ministry of Foreign Affairs of the
People's Republic of China

Wang Yu-tang
Member of the Committee
Responsible Member of the Office
for the Organization of the
Exhibition of Archaeological
Finds, State Administrative
Bureau of Museums and Archaeological
Data

Kuo Lao-wei
Member of the Committee
Head of the Department of Foreign
Affairs
State Administrative Bureau of
Museums and Archaeological Data

Wang Cheng-li
Member of the Committee
Assistant-Curator of the Museum
of Kirin Province

THE UNITED STATES COMMITTEE FOR THE
EXHIBITION OF THE ARCHAEOLOGICAL FINDS OF
THE PEOPLE'S REPUBLIC OF CHINA OF THE
NATIONAL GALLERY OF ART OF THE UNITED STATES
OF AMERICA

J. Carter Brown, Chairman
Director
National Gallery of Art

René-Yvon Lefebvre d'Argencé
Director and Chief Curator
Asian Art Museum of San Francisco

Laurence Sickman
Director
The Nelson Gallery-Atkins Museum

Alexander Eckstein
Brookings Institution

Alex B. Lacy
Deputy Director
Division of Public Programs
National Endowment for the
Humanities

Thomas Lawton
Assistant Director
Freer Gallery of Art

Arthur H. Rosen
President
National Committee on United States-China
Relations, Inc.

Peter Solmssen
Advisor on the Arts
Bureau of Educational & Cultural
Affairs
Department of State

Harold P. Stern
Director
Freer Gallery of Art

Murray Zinoman
China Program Officer
Bureau of Educational & Cultural
Affairs
Department of State

FOREWORD

A few years ago, word reached this country of the recent extraordinary archaeological discoveries that had been made throughout The People's Republic of China - finds that were not only of great archaeological interest but often of incomparable beauty. These exceptional objects, spanning some 600,000 years of China's past, have been shown in Washington and Kansas City and are now on display in the Asian Art Museum of San Francisco.

For this rare privilege, we wish to express our profound thanks and gratitude to the people and the Government of The People's Republic of China who, in their deep concern with the preservation and display of their country's cultural heritage, have so generously lent to the American public these newly excavated national treasures.

Many people were involved in the realization of this exhibition, and we owe each our deep appreciation for their generous expenditure of time and effort. The names of many of them are to be found on those committees listed elsewhere in this catalogue.

We are particularly grateful to the Committee for the Organization of Exhibitions of Archaeological Finds of The People's Republic of China. This committee selected the objects for the exhibition, and was of invaluable aid during its early planning stages. We should like to record our gratitude to the Chinese Exhibition Council of London for much assistance, and particularly to its chairman, Lord Trevelyan.

To all those countries which have played host to the exhibition - France, England, Austria, Sweden, and Canada - and to those who have worked with us to make the exhibition a reality, must go our sincere appreciation.

We are very grateful to the National Endowment for the Humanities and various local sponsors (listed on a separate page in this catalogue) for their generous support of our undertaking.

The National Gallery of Art, The Nelson Gallery-Atkins Museum and the Asian Art Museum of San Francisco are proud and honored to bring to you The Exhibition of Archaeological Finds of The People's Republic of China. We commend it to your interest and pleasure.

René-Yvon Lefebvre d'Argencé
Director and Chief Curator
Asian Art Museum of San Francisco

Laurence Sickman
Director
The Nelson Gallery-Atkins Museum

J. Carter Brown
Director
National Gallery of Art

COMPARATIVE CHRONOLOGY

CHINA	WESTERN AND OTHER
PRIMITIVE SOCIETY (c. 600,000-4,000 BC) Lantian Man (c. 600,000 BC)	Pebble-tool Culture ⎱ (c. 600,000 BC) Heidelberg Man ⎰ Neanderthal Man (c. 200,000 BC) Cro-Magnon Man (c. 35,000 BC)
SLAVE SOCIETY (c. 21st century-475 BC)	Great Pyramids in Egypt (c. 2500 BC)
HSIA DYNASTY (c. 21st-16th c. BC)	
SHANG DYNASTY (c. 16th-11th c. BC)	Stonehenge (c. 2000-1400 BC) Trojan War (c. 1200 BC)
WESTERN CHOU (c. 11th c.-770 BC)	Homer (8th c. BC)
SPRING AND AUTUMN PERIOD (c. 770-476 BC)	Rome founded (? 753 BC)
FEUDAL SOCIETY (475 BC-1840 AD)	
WARRING STATES PERIOD (475-221 BC)	Buddha (c. 560-c. 480 BC) Plato (c. 428-347 BC) Aristotle (c. 384-322 BC) Alexander the Great (336-323 BC)
CHIN DYNASTY (221-207 BC) Capital at Hsienyang (near Sian)	Hannibal crosses the Alps (218 BC)
WESTERN HAN DYNASTY (206 BC-24 AD) Capital at Changan (Sian)	Julius Caesar (? 104-44 BC)
EASTERN HAN DYNASTY (25-220 AD) Capital at Loyang	Jesus Christ (? 4 BC-30 AD)
THE THREE KINGDOMS (220-265 AD) *Wei* (220-265 AD) Capital at Loyang *Shu* (221-263 AD) Capital at Chengtu *Wu* (222-280 AD) Capital at Chienyeh (Nanking)	
WESTERN TSIN DYNASTY (265-316 AD) Capital at Loyang	Partition of Roman Empire (285 AD)
EASTERN TSIN DYNASTY (317-420 AD) Capital at Chienkang (Nanking)	Rome adopts Christianity (340 AD)
SOUTHERN DYNASTIES (420-589 AD) Capital at Chienkang (Nanking)	
NORTHERN DYNASTIES (386-581 AD) *Northern Wei Dynasty* (386-534 AD) Capital at Tatung, later at Loyang *Eastern Wei Dynasty* (534-549 AD) Capital at Yeh (Anyang)	Sack of Rome (410 AD)

CHINA	WESTERN AND OTHER
Western Wei Dynasty (535-556 AD) Capital at Changan (Sian)	
Northern Chi Dynasty (550-577 AD) Capital at Yeh (Anyang)	Silkworms introduced into Europe (552 AD)
Northern Chou Dynasty (557-581 AD) Capital at Changan (Sian)	Mohammed (570-632 AD)
SUI DYNASTY (581-618 AD) Capital at Tahsing (Sian)	
TANG DYNASTY (618-907 AD) Capital at Changan (Sian)	Charlemagne (768-814 AD)
FIVE DYNASTIES (907-960 AD)	
SUNG DYNASTY (960-1279 AD) *Northern Sung Dynasty* (960-1127 AD) Capital at Kaifeng *Southern Sung Dynasty* (1127-1279 AD) Capital at Linan (Hangchow)	Leif Ericsson (1000 AD) Norman Conquest of England (1066 AD) Paper first manufactured in Europe (1150 AD) Magna Carta (1215 AD)
LIAO DYNASTY (916-1125 AD) Capital at Linhuang (Barin Left Banner)	
KIN DYNASTY (1115-1234 AD) Capital at Huining (Acheng)	Genghis Khan (1206-1227 AD)
YUAN DYNASTY (1271-1368 AD) Capital at Tatu (Peking)	Gunpowder introduced in Europe (1313 AD)
MING DYNASTY (1368-1644 AD) Capital at Nanking, later at Peking	
CHING DYNASTY (1644-1840 AD, down to the 20th year of the reign of Taokuang) Capital at Peking	

CLASSIFICATION OF BRONZE VESSELS

Principal types of ceremonial vessels with their neolithic ceramic antecedent forms together with the appropriate old characters and their modern equivalents

Vessels for	Food					Water	
Type	li	ting	hsien	kuei	tou	p'an	chien
Primary form							
Old character and modern equivalent							
Neolithic antecedent form							

Prepared for the exhibit in Vienna, based on the research of William Willets, Das Buch der Chinesischen Kunst, Dusseldorf-Wien, 1968, p. 96-f.

				Wine				
yu	hu	lei	fang-yi	chia	chüeh	ku	ho	kuang
卣	壺	罍	彝	斝	爵		盉	

COLOR PLATES

Numerals refer to exhibit numbers

29

36

70

80

89

87

95

133

164, 165

145

168

265 — 272

274

277

369

370

EXHIBITS

I / Excavations of the Sites of Lantian Man and Peking Man

(about 600,000—400,000 years ago)

1

1. Skull and lower jaw of
   Lantian Man (model)
   Cranium: Unearthed in 1964 at
                Kungwangling village,
                Lantian, Shensi
   Lower jaw: Unearthed in 1963 at
                Chenchiawo village,
                Lantian, Shensi

2. Bust of Lantian Man
   (restoration)
   Made in 1972 by the Institute of
   Vertebrate Palentology and
   Paleoanthropology of the
   Chinese Academy of Sciences

2

3

4

5

3. Pointed tool of quartzite
   (used by Lantian man)
   (reproduction)
   Length 17.5 cm.
   Unearthed in 1965 at Kungwangling village,
   Lantian, Shensi

4. Scraper of vein quartz
   (used by Lantian man)
   (reproduction)
   Length 2.8 cm.
   Unearthed in 1965 at Kungwangling village,
   Lantian Shensi

5. Skull of Peking Man (model)
   Unearthed in 1966 at Locality I of
   Choukoutien, Peking

6. Lower jaw of Peking Man (model)
   Unearthed in 1959 at Locality I
   of Choukoutien, Peking

6

Tools used by Peking Man and evidence of use of fire by Peking Man, unearthed in 1966 at Locality I of Choukoutien, Peking

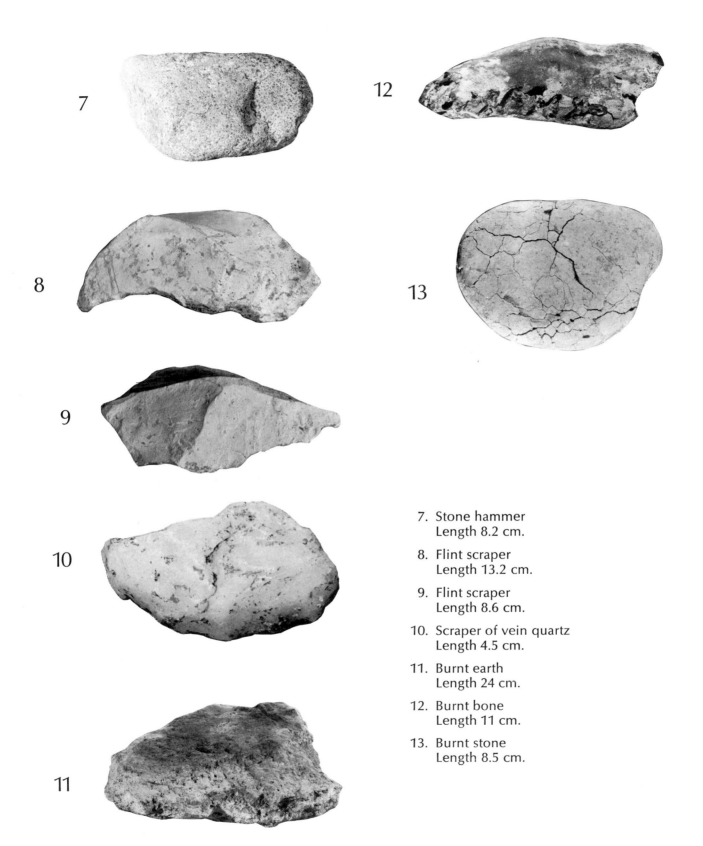

7. Stone hammer
   Length 8.2 cm.

8. Flint scraper
   Length 13.2 cm.

9. Flint scraper
   Length 8.6 cm.

10. Scraper of vein quartz
    Length 4.5 cm.

11. Burnt earth
    Length 24 cm.

12. Burnt bone
    Length 11 cm.

13. Burnt stone
    Length 8.5 cm.

II / Yangshao Culture Site at Panpo Village, Sian, Shensi Province, Unearthed between 1954 and 1957

(about 6,000 years ago)

Panpo Village during excavation

14

15

14. Stone axe
    Length 12 cm.

15. Stone chisel
    Length 8 cm.

16

17

18

16. Stone adze
    Length 6 cm.

17. Bone spade
    Length 11 cm.

18. Bone chisel .
    Length 14 cm.

19. Bone harpoon head
    Length 14.8 cm.

19

20. Bone arrow head
    Length 6.1 cm.

21. Bone hairpin
    Length 16 cm.

22. Bone needle
    Length 16.5 cm.

20

21

22

23

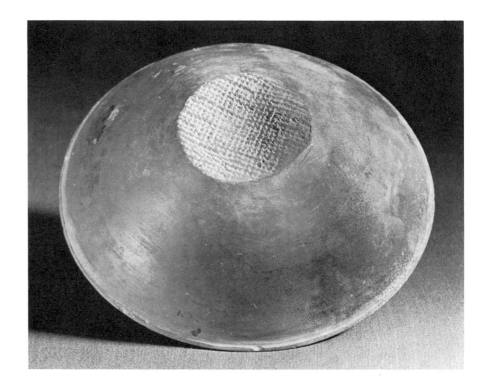

24

23. Stone whorl
    Diameter 3.8 cm.

24. Pottery bowl (with textile impressions
    on bottom)
    Height 4 cm., dia. of mouth 13 cm.

25. Pottery bowl (with matting impressions
    on bottom)
    Height 10.5 cm., dia. of mouth 24 cm.

25

26

27

26. Pottery jar with stippling
    Height 11 cm.

27. Pottery jar with finger-nail
    impressions
    Height 15 cm.

28

30

29

28. Pottery amphora with pointed bottom
    Height 43 cm.

29. Pottery basin painted with human-mask design
    Height 17 cm., dia. of mouth 44.5 cm.

30. Pottery basin painted with deer design
    Height 17 cm., dia. of mouth 42.8 cm.

31

32

31. Pottery bowl painted with triangle design
    Height 9 cm., dia. of mouth 14.5 cm.

32. Pottery jar painted with triangle design
    Height 12.7 cm.

33

33. Painted pottery waisted jar
    Height 18.3 cm.
    Unearthed in 1958 at Lanchow, Kansu

34. Painted pottery *tou* (stemmed bowl) with wave design
Height 16.4 cm.
Unearthed in 1958 at
Lanchow, Kansu

35. Pottery basin painted with curved lines
Height 9.5 cm., dia. of mouth 23 cm.
Unearthed in 1966 at
Lanchow, Kansu

34

35

36. Painted pottery amphora with
flat bottom
Height 38 cm.
Unearthed in 1958 at
Kanku, Kansu

37. Painted pottery vase with four circles filled
in with geometric pattern
Height 49 cm.
Unearthed in 1956 at Yungching, Kansu

37

IV / Chinglienkang Culture
(about 5,000 years ago)

38. Perforated stone axe
Length 15 cm.
Unearthed in 1956 at
Nanking, Kiangsu

39

40

39. Stone knife with seven holes
    Length 22.6 cm.
    Unearthed in 1956 at Nanking, Kiangsu

40. Stone stepped adze
    Length 17.3 cm.
    Unearthed in 1953 at Wuhsien, Kiangsu

41. Stone hoe
    Length 13.5 cm.
    Unearthed in 1955 at Nanking, Kiangsu

41

42

43

44

42. Bone chisel
Length 16.3 cm.
Unearthed in 1960 at Wukiang, Kiangsu

43. Bone harpoon
Length 16.5 cm.
Unearthed in 1960 at Wukiang, Kiangsu

44. Bone arrow head
Length 16 cm.
Unearthed in 1960 at Wukiang, Kiangsu

45. Bone needle
Length 18.1 cm.
Unearthed in 1960 at Wukiang, Kiangsu

45

46. *Chueh* ring (penannular) of white jade
Diameter 6.2 cm.
Unearthed in 1956 at Nanking, Kiangsu

47. *Huang* (half-ring) of green nephrite
Length 12.6 cm.
Unearthed in 1955 at Nanking, Kiangsu

48. Painted pottery bowl
Height 10 cm., dia. of mouth 18 cm.
Unearthed in 1966 at Peihsien, Kiangsu

46

47

48

49. Painted pottery vase with
    flower-petal design
    Height 19.5 cm.
    Unearthed in 1966 at Peihsien,
    Kiangsu

50. Pottery basin painted with
    flower-petal design
    Height 16.5 cm., dia. of mouth
    30.2 cm.
    Unearthed in 1966 at Peihsien,
    Kiangsu

49

50

51. Pottery basin painted with eight-point
    star design
    Height 18.5 cm., dia. of mouth 33.8 cm.
    Unearthed in 1963 at Peihsien, Kiangsu

51

52. Red pottery tripod *kuei* (pitcher)
    Height 31.8 cm.
    Unearthed in 1960

53. White pottery tripod *kuei* (pitcher)
    Height 29.7 cm.
    Unearthed in 1960

52

53

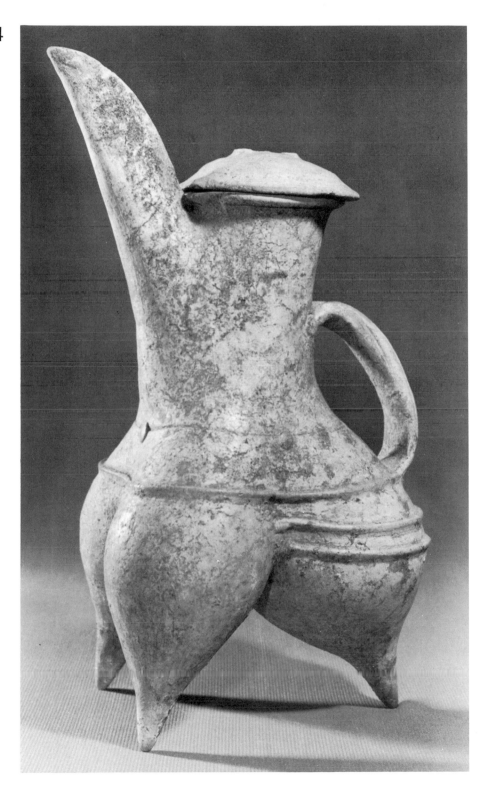

54

54. White pottery *ho* (kettle)
    Height 31 cm.
    Unearthed in 1964

55

56. Black pottery cup with two ears
Height 12.5 cm.
Unearthed in 1960

56. Black pottery *tou* (stemmed cup) with thin body
Height 16.3 cm.
Unearthed in 1960

56

58

57. Black pottery tripod *ting*
    Height 15 cm.
    Unearthed in 1960

58. Black pottery stemmed plate
    Height 18.7 cm., dia. 43.8 cm.
    Unearthed in 1960

57

VI / Shang Dynasty Site at Chengchow, Honan Province
(16th - 11th century B.C.)

59. Bronze *ko* with whorl design
   Length 20.3 cm.
   Unearthed in 1954

60. Bronze spear head
   Length 18.5 cm.
   Unearthed in 1954

60

59

61

62

64

63

61. Bronze arrow head
    Length 6.7 cm.
    Unearthed in 1953

62. Bronze arrow head
    Length 6.5 cm.
    Unearthed in 1954

63. Bronze knife
    Length 25.6 cm.
    Unearthed in 1954

64. Dark green nephrite *ko* (halberd)
    Length 38 cm.
    Unearthed in 1955

65

66

68

67

69

65. Bone arrow head
    Length 9.5 cm.
    Unearthed in 1955

66. Bone *pi* (spatula)
    Length 11 cm.
    Unearthed in 1954

67. Bone comb
    Length 10.1 cm.
    Unearthed in 1954

68. Bone hairpin
    Length 15.3 cm.
    Unearthed in 1955

69. Thigh bone of an ox
    sawed for making artifacts
    Length 14 cm.
    Unearthed in 1955

70

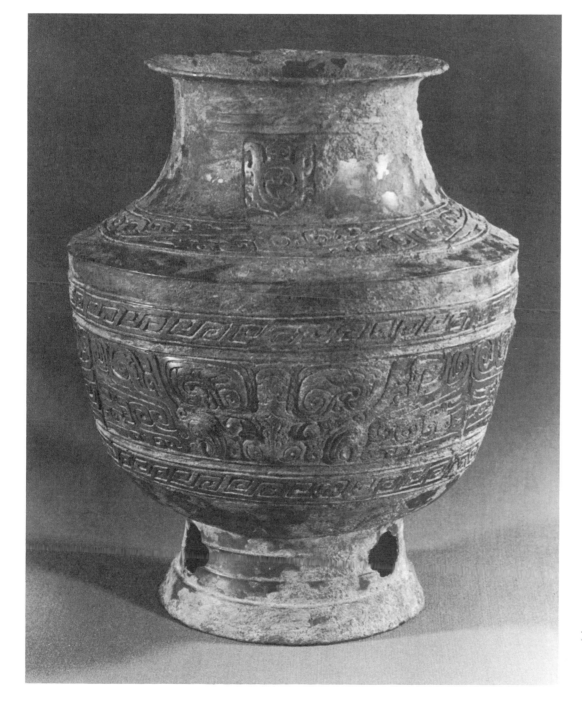

70. Bronze *lei* with animal-mask
design
Height 25 cm.
Unearthed in 1955

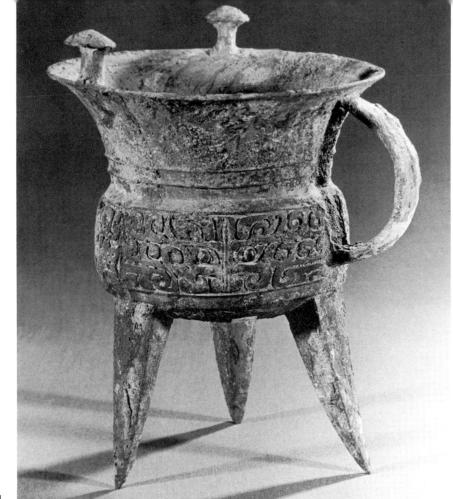

71. Bronze tripod *chia* with animal-mask design
    Height 22 cm.
    Unearthed in 1955

72. Bronze tripod *ting* with animal-mask design
    Height 19 cm.
    Unearthed in 1955

71

72

73. Bronze *pan* with *kuei* dragon design
    Height 10.5 cm., dia. of mouth 30 cm.
    Unearthed in 1955

73

74

74. Bronze *tsun* with animal-mask design
    Height 24.9 cm.
    Unearthed in 1954

75. Bronze tripod *li* with *kuei* dragon design
    Height 16.5 cm.
    Unearthed in 1955

75

76

76. Bronze *ku* with animal-mask design
    Height 18 cm.
    Unearthed in 1965

77. Bronze *chueh* with animal-mask design
    Height 17.2 cm.
    Unearthed in 1965

77

78

78. Large mouthed *tsun*
(wine container) of proto-porcelain
Height 28.2 cm.
Unearthed in 1965

79. Pottery *yen*
Height 40 cm.
Unearthed in 1953

80. Pottery *tsun*
Height 34.5 cm.
Unearthed in 1954

79

80

VII / Yin Ruins at Anyang, Honan Province
(14th — 11th century B.C.)

81

82

81 Bronze *yu*, inscribed "Pei Kan (?)"
   12th century B.C.
   Height including handle 29 cm.
   Unearthed in 1950 from the large tomb at Wukuan
   village, Anyang, Honan

82. Bronze *kuei*, inscribed "Pei Kan (?) Ko"
   12th century B.C.
   Height 14.3 cm., dia. of mouth 20.7 cm.
   Unearthed in 1950 from the large tomb at Wukuan
   village, Anyang, Honan

83

83. Bronze tripod *ting,* inscribed "Fu Chi"
    11th century B.C.
    Height 21.7 cm.
    Unearthed in 1950 at Anyang, Honan

84. Bronze tripod *chia*, inscribed "Mu Ya"
12th century B.C.
Height 30.8 cm.
Unearthed in 1959 at Anyang, Honan

84

85

86

85. Inscription on ox shoulder blade
    14th century B.C.
    Length 40.5 cm.
    Unearthed in 1971 at Anyang, Honan

86. Inscription on ox shoulder blade
    14th century B.C.
    Length 37 cm.
    Unearthed in 1971 at Anyang, Honan

VIII / Shang Dynasty Bronzes from Shansi, Anhwei and Hunan Provinces
(12th — 11th century B.C.)

FRONT VIEW

87. Owl-shaped bronze *yu*
    11th century B.C.
    Height 19.7 cm.
    Unearthed in 1957 at Shihlou, Shansi

87

SIDE VIEW

88

88. Bronze *kuang* with dragon design
11th century B.C.
Length 41.5 cm.
Unearthed in 1959 at Shihlou, Shansi

88 B

88. Bronze *kuang* with dragon design
    11th century B.C.
    Length 41.5 cm.
    Unearthed in 1959 at Shihlou, Shansi

88 C

89. Bronze *tsun* with animal-mask design
    12th — 11th century B.C.
    Height 47 cm.
    Unearthed in 1957 at Funan, Anhwei

90. Bronze tripod *chia* with animal-mask design
    12th century B.C.
    Height 55.3 cm.
    Unearthed in 1965 at Feihsi, Anhwei

91. Bronze *ting* with human-mask design, inscribed ''Ta Ho''
11th century B.C.
Height 38.7 cm.
Unearthed in 1959 at Ninghsiang, Hunan

92. Bronze square *tsun* with animal-mask decoration
11th century B.C.
Height 53.8 cm.
Unearthed in 1963 at Changning, Hunan

91

92

WESTERN CHOU DYNASTY
(11th century — 770 B.C.)

IX / Western Chou Bronzes from Chichia Village, Fufeng, Shensi Province
(10th — 9th century B.C.)

93

93. Bronze *kuang* marked "Jih Chi"
10th century B.C.
Height 31.6 cm.
Unearthed in 1963

94. Bronze square *tsun* marked "Jih Chi"
10th century B.C.
Height 29.5 cm.
Unearthed in 1963

作文考日己寶
尊宗彝其子孫
萬年永寶用大

95. Bronze square *yi* marked "Jih Ch
10th century B.C.
Height 38.5 cm.
Unearthed in 1963

96. Bronze *ho* with bird-shaped lid
    10th century B.C.
    Height 38 cm.
    Unearthed in 1963

97. Bronze *hu* marked "Chi Fu"
10th — 9th century B.C.
Height 59.4 cm.
Unearthed in 1960

隹五月初
吉庚午同仲容
西宮易戲父示
茅六僕四家金
十鈞戲父丼頯
首對揚朕皇君
休用作朕剌考
尊壺戲父用追
孝其萬年孫：
子永寶用

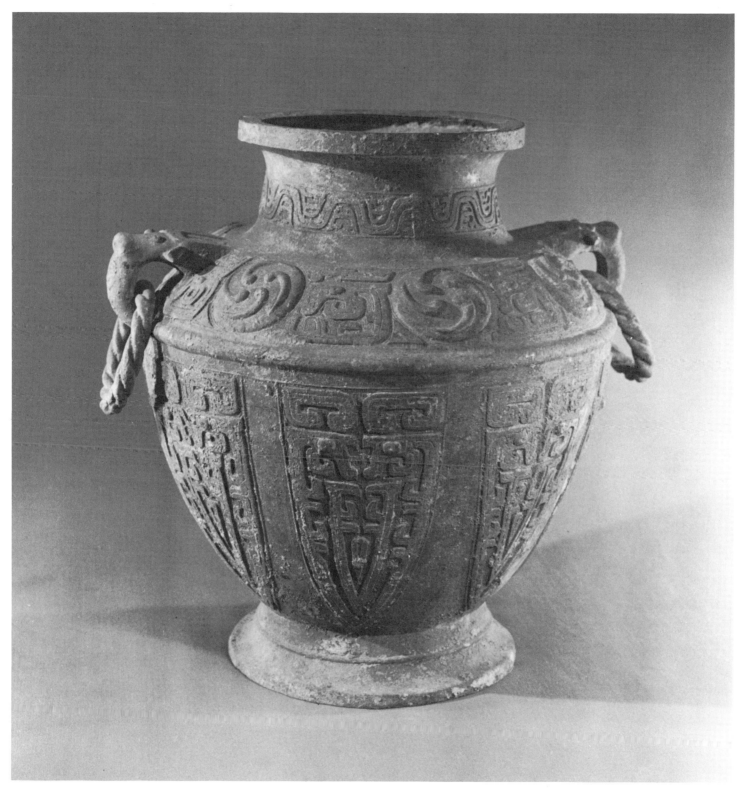

98. Bronze *lei* with *kuei* dragon design
10th — 9th century B.C.
Height 46.1 cm.
Unearthed in 1960

父　史
壬　戌
尊　作

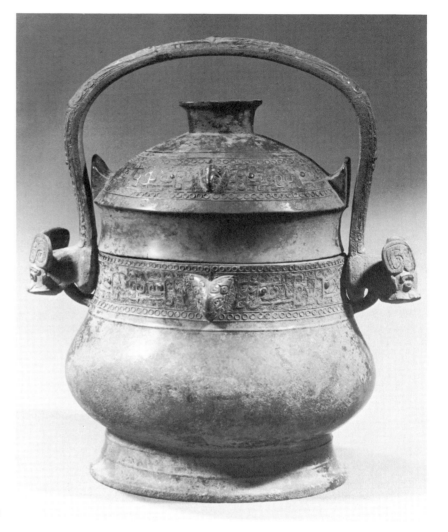

99. Bronze *kuei* marked "Yu Fu Kuei"
Height 16.7 cm., dia. of mouth 25 cm.

100. Bronze *yu* marked "Shih Hsu"
Height including handle 28.5 cm.

100

99

101. Bronze *yu* marked "Kung"
     Height including handle 23.5 cm.
     Unearthed in 1965

101

公作寶尊彝

其孫子永用

102. Bronze *kuei* decorated with
     stylized animal-mask design
     Height 19.7 cm., dia. of mouth 27.2 cm.
     Unearthed in 1965

103

103. Bronze *pan* with *kuei* dragon design
Height 9.4 cm., dia. of mouth 31.6 cm.
Unearthed in 1959

105

104. Proto-porcelain vase with three ears
Height 11 cm.
Unearthed in 1965

105. Proto-porcelain *tsun* (wine vessel) with two ears
Height 11.9 cm.
Unearthed in 1965

106. Proto-porcelain vase with two ears
Height 15 cm.
Unearthed in 1965

106

XII / Bronzes of the Spring and Autumn Period
from Anhwei and Shansi Provinces
(5th century B.C.)

107-115. Bronze *pien chung* (chime of bells)
of the Marquis of Tsai
Height 16.6 - 28 cm.
Unearthed in 1955 at Shouhsien, Anhwei

116. Bronze tripod *ting* in the shape of a sacrificial animal
Height 27.5 cm.
Unearthed in 1959 at Shucheng, Anhwei

117

117. Bronze rectangular *hu* with interlaced dragon design
     Height 86.6 cm.
     Unearthed in 1961 at Houma, Shansi

118. Bronze *chien* with interlaced hydras design
     Height 36.8 cm., dia. of mouth 76 cm.
     Unearthed in 1961 at Houma, Shansi

118

XIII / Surverys and Excavations of City Sites of the Warring States Period
(4th century B.C.)

119

119. Bronze knocker ornamented
with interlaced hydras and
phoenix design
Length of animal mask 45.5 cm.,
dia. of ring 29 cm.
Unearthed in 1966 at Yihsien,
Hopei

121

120. Semi-cylindrical tile with cicada pattern
    Length 54.5 cm.
    Unearthed in 1966 at Yihsien, Hopei

121. Semi-circular tile-end with animal-mask design
    Length 33.5 cm., dia. 23 cm.
    Unearthed in 1964 at Yihsien, Hopei

122. Semi-circular tile-end with animal-mask design
    Length 14 cm., dia. 28 cm.
    Unearthed in 1964 at Yihsien, Hopei

120

122

123

124

123. Iron mould and core for casting an axe, inscribed "Right Granary"
Length of mould 28.6 cm., length of core 21.9 cm.

124. Iron mould for casting a pair of sickles, inscribed "Right Granary"
Length 32.5 cm.

XV / Chu Tombs at Chiangling, Hupeh Province
(5th century B.C.)

125-126. Dragon-shaped jade ornaments
Length 28 cm.
Unearthed in 1965

127. Bronze sword with lozenge design
Length 60.8 cm.
Unearthed in 1965

125

126

127

128. Bronze *tsun* (wine vessel)
with stylized dragon design
Height 17.1 cm.
Unearthed in 1965

129. Iron belt-hook with gold inlay
Length 46.3 cm.
Unearthed in 1965

128

129

131

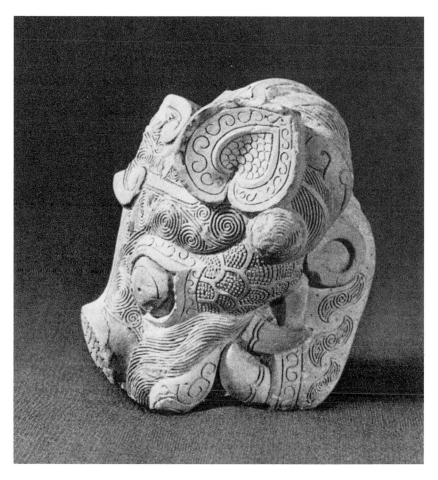

130. Pottery mould for casting a figure of a tiger
     Length 18.5 cm.
     Unearthed in 1959 at Houma, Shansi

131. Pottery model for making mould of animal-head
     Height 10.9 cm.
     Unearthed in 1960 at Houma, Shansi

130

132. Pottery relief model for making a mould of an
     animal-mask design
     Length 32.8 cm.
     Unearthed in 1960 at Houma, Shansi

133. Bronze *tou* inlaid with gold in *kuei* dragon design
     Height 19.2 cm.
     Unearthed in 1965 at Changchih, Shansi

133

134

134. Bronze rim of a vessel inlaid with gold and silver
Diameter 12 cm.
Unearthed in 1954 at Hochin, Shansi

135. Bronze ornament with silver inlay
Length 21.3 cm.
Unearthed in 1954 at Yungchi, Shansi

136. Bronze ewer with eagle's head
Height 47.5 cm.
Unearthed in 1970 at Chucheng, Shantung

135

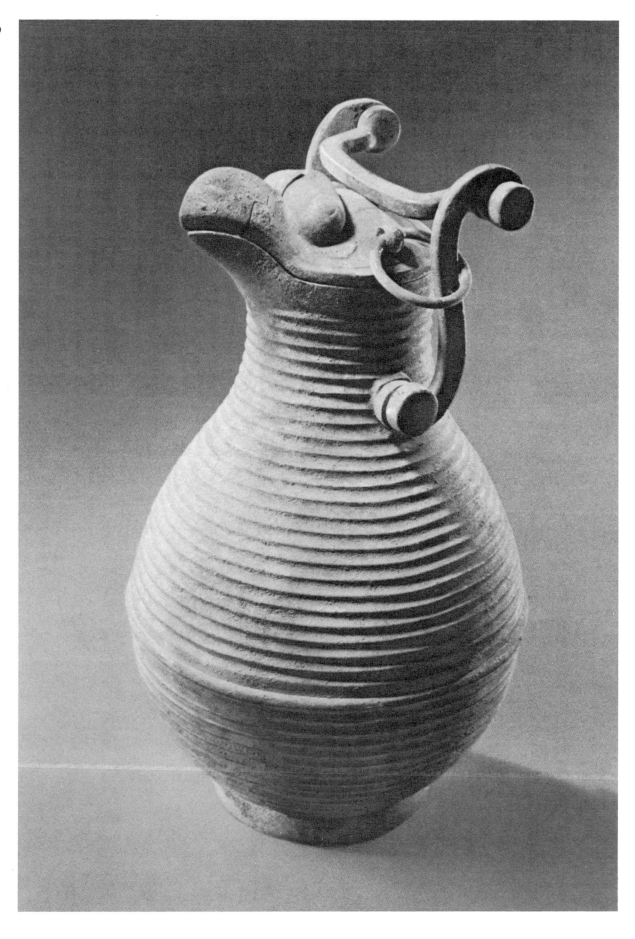

秦 **CHIN DYNASTY**
(221 — 207 B.C.)

XVII / Cultural Relics of the Chin Dynasty from Shensi and Shantung Provinces
(3rd century B.C.)

137

138

137. Pottery measure, inscribed
Height 9.4 cm., dia. of mouth 20.4 cm.
Unearthed in 1963 at Tsouhsien, Shantung

138. Brick stamped with a hunting scene
Length 47.5 cm.
Unearthed in 1957 at Lintung, Shensi

139. Pottery figure of a squatting woman
Height 64.5 cm.
Unearthed in 1964 at Lintung, Shensi

139

XVIII / The Tombs of Liu Sheng, Prince Ching of Chungshan, of the Western Han Dynasty and of His Wife, Tou Wan, unearthed in 1968 at Mancheng, Hopei Province

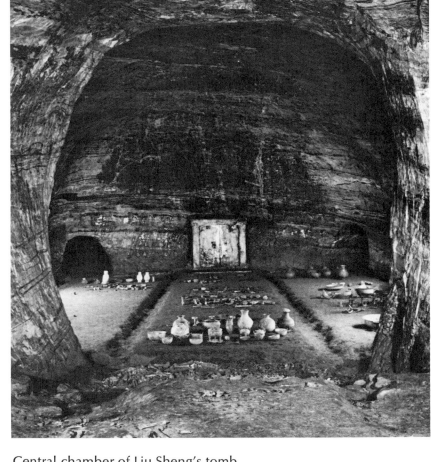

Central chamber of Liu Sheng's tomb

140. Bronze *chuan* (water container) inscribed "Household of the Prince of Chungshan" Height 13 cm., dia. of mouth 28.1 cm. Unearthed from the tomb of Tou Wan

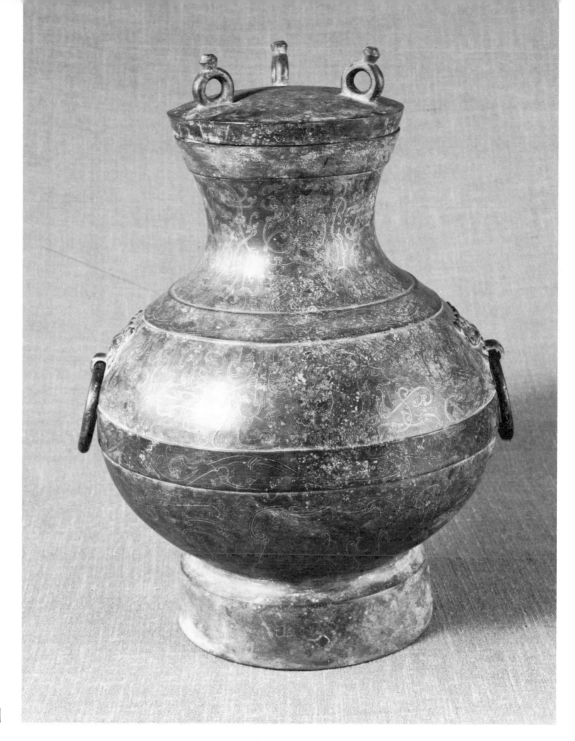

141

Section of bird script inlay redrawn

141. Bronze *hu* (wine vessel) with gold and silver inlay of
      bird script
      Height 40 cm.
      Unearthed from the tomb of Tou Wan

142. Bronze *hu* (wine vessel) inlaid with gold and silver
Height 59 cm.
Unearthed from the tomb of Liu Sheng

143. Bronze lamp in the form of a ram
Height of ram 18.6 cm., length 23 cm.
Unearthed from the tomb of Liu Sheng

143

144. Bronze lamp with stand inscribed
"Household of Prince of Chungshan"
Height of lamp 5.2 cm., dia. of
stand 22.1 cm.
Unearthed from the tomb of Tou Wan

145. Bronze lamp with shade
Height 32.8 cm.
Unearthed from the tomb of Liu Sheng

146. Bronze *poshan* censer
supported by a human
figure mounted on a
beast
Height 32.4 cm.
Unearthed from the
tomb of Tou Wan

147

147. Jade suit, sewn with gold thread; shroud
for Tou Wan, wife of Prince Ching of
Chungshan
Length 172 cm.
Unearthed from the tomb of Tou Wan

Detail, 147

148. Gilt bronze headrest inlaid
     with jade
     Length 41.3 cm.
     Unearthed from the tomb of
     Tou Wan

148

149, 150

149, 150. Jade *huang* (crescent-shaped ritual object)
(2 pieces)
Length of smaller 13 cm., length of
larger 13.7 cm.
Unearthed from the tomb of Tou Wan

151. Tou Wan's bronze seal (reproduction)
2 cm. square, 0.7 cm. thick
Unearthed from the tomb of Tou Wan

152-157. Jade *pi* discs
Diameter 14.1 cm. — 21.2 cm.
Unearthed from the tomb of Tou Wan

152—157

158. Iron knife with hilt-ring bound with gold wire
Length 25.7 cm.
Unearthed from the tomb of Liu Sheng

159. Bronze dagger
Length 28.1 cm.
Unearthed from the tomb of Liu Sheng

160. Bronze sword
Length 72.5 cm.
Unearthed from the tomb of Liu Sheng

161. Bronze *ko* (halberd) with gilt bird-shaped ornament
Length 20 cm.
Unearthed from the tomb of Liu Sheng

162. Gold acupuncture needle
Length 6.5 cm.
Unearthed from the tomb of Liu Sheng

163. Silver acupuncture needle
Length 7.1 cm.
Unearthed from the tomb of Liu Sheng

164

165

164, 165. Bronze leopards inlaid with gold
        Height 3.5 cm.
        Unearthed from the tomb of Liu Sheng

166, 167. Bronze feet of vessel in shape of bears
           and birds
           Height 11.4 cm. and 11.7 cm.
           Unearthed from the tomb of Liu Sheng

168. Pottery basin painted with fish design
Height 14.7 cm., dia. of mouth 55.5 cm.
Unearthed from the tomb of Liu Sheng

168

169

169. Bronze ploughshare
Length 30 cm.
Unearthed in 1956

170. Bronze axe ornamented
with two birds
Height 21 cm.
Unearthed in 1956

170

171. Bronze mandarin duck
Height 11.2 cm.
Unearthed in 1956

Detail, 172

171

172. Bronze cowrie-container decorated with
weaving scene on lid
Height 27.5 cm., dia. of bottom 30.9 cm.
Unearthed in 1955

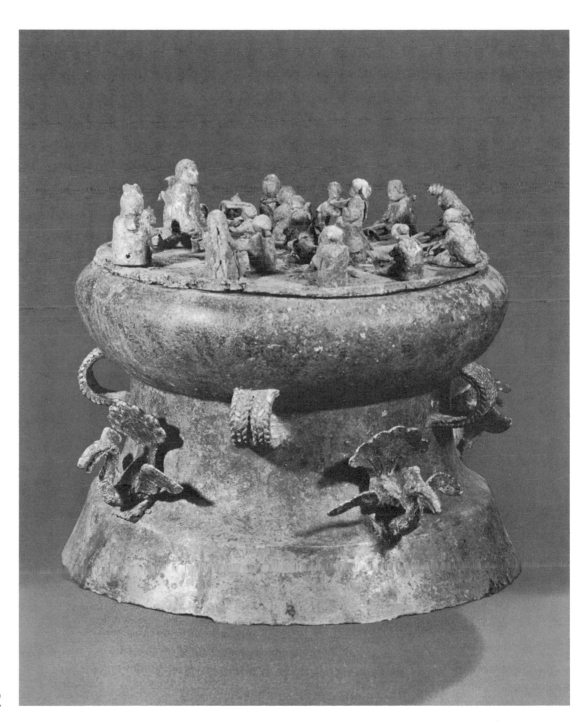

173. Bronze ornament in form of
buffalo heads and bulls
Width 11.2 cm.
Unearthed in 1956

174. Bronze ornament in form of
boar struggling with two tigers
Length 17.1 cm.
Unearthed in 1956

173

174

175. Bronze deer
     Height 15.6 cm.
     Unearthed in 1956

176. Bronze peacock
     Height 14.4 cm.
     Unearthed in 1956

177—192

177-192. Agate and carnelian bead
    Length 1.1 cm. - 7.3 cm.
    Unearthed in 1956

193-198. Agate and carnelian
    button-shaped
    ornaments
    Diameter 4.4 cm. - 5.8 cm.
    Unearthed in 1956

193—198

199, 200. Two painted pottery horsemen
2nd century B.C.
Height 65 cm. and 68.5 cm.
Unearthed in 1965 at Hsienyang, Shensi

199

200

201. Bronze *fang hu* (square wine vessel) inlaid
     with gold in hydras design
     Height 61 cm.
     Unearthed in 1964 at Sian, Shensi

202. Silver-inlaid bronze *tsun* (wine vessel)
in the form of a sacrificial animal
2nd century B.C.
Height 27.4 cm., length 41.8 cm.
Unearthed in 1965 at Lienshui, Kiangsu

203

203. Bronze chariot ornament inlaid with
     gold and silver
     1st century B.C.
     Length 26.5 cm.
     Unearthed in 1965 at Tinghsien, Hopei

204. Bronze *tsun* (wine vessel) gilded and
     with silver decoration, inscribed
     26 B.C.
     Height 34.7 cm., dia. of mouth 65.5 cm.
     Unearthed in 1962 at Yuyu, Shansi

204

205

206

205. Gilded bronze *tsun* for warming wine
26 B.C.
Height 24.5 cm., dia. of mouth 23.4 cm.
Unearthed in 1962 at Yuyu, Shansi

206. Painted pottery vase
1st century B.C.
Height 49.5 cm.
Unearthed in 1957 at Loyang, Honan

207. Pottery model of a courtyard
1st century A.D.
Height 76 cm., width 93 cm.
Unearthed in 1959 at Chengchow, Honan

207

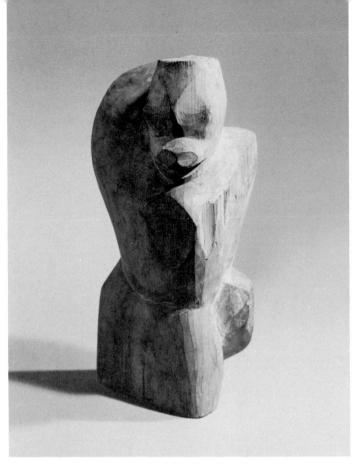

208. Painted wooden unicorn
2nd century A.D.
Height 38.5 cm., length 59 cm.
Unearthed in 1959 at Wuwei, Kansu

209. Wooden monkey
2nd century A.D.
Height 32.5 cm.
Unearthed in 1957 at Wuwei, Kansu

209

208

211

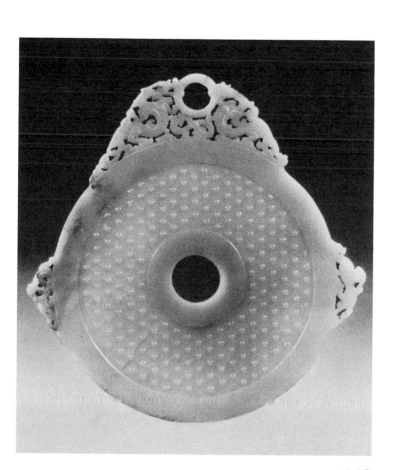

210

210. *Pi* disc of green nephrite decorated with
animal design and ring
1st century A.D.
Height 30 cm.
Unearthed in 1969 at Tinghsien, Hopei

211. *Pi* disc of green nephrite decorated
with hydras design
1st century A.D.
Height 25.5 cm.
Unearthed in 1959 at Tinghsien, Hopei

212 - 217. Six pottery figures of musicians and
dancers
1st century A.D.
Height 15 cm. — 15.5 cm.
Unearthed in 1965 at Loyang, Honan

212 — 217

XXI / Bronze Figurines, Chariots, and Horses from an Eastern Han Tomb in Wuwei, Kansu Province, Unearthed in 1969
(2nd century A.D.)

218. Bronze galloping horse
Height 34.5 cm., length 45 cm.

218

219, 220. Two bronze horses
Height 36.5 cm. and 38 cm.

219, 220

221

221. Bronze horseman
Height 39 cm.

222. Bronze horseman armed with halberd
Height 52.3 cm.

223. Bronze horseman armed with spear
Height 53 cm.

223

222

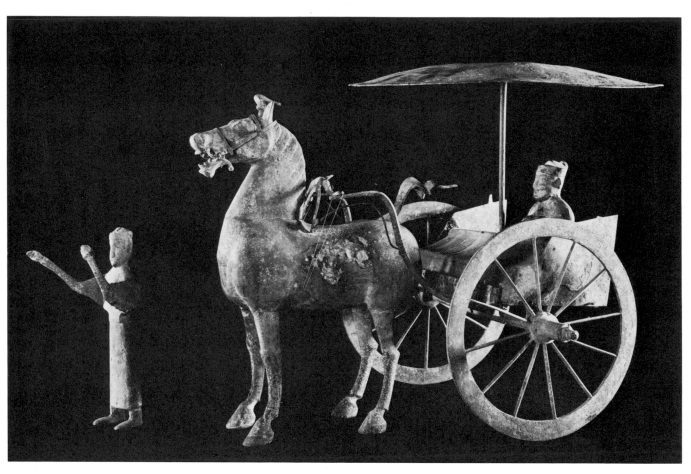

228 — 231

224 - 227. Bronze chariot mounted
with ax (a chariot, a horse, and
two figurines)
Height of horse 40 cm., length
of chariot 33 cm.

228 - 231. Bronze yao chariot (a
chariot, a horse, and two
figurines)
Height of horse 40 cm., height
of chariot 43.5 cm.

224 — 227

232 - 234. Bronze *chu* cart (a cart, a horse, and a figurine)
Height of horse 38 cm., length of
cart 63 cm.

235. Procession scene, part of the wall-painting
of an Eastern Han tomb (copy)
170 x 327 cm.
Discovered in 1971 at Anping, Hopei

232 — 234

235

两晋南北朝

THE THREE KINGDOMS, THE WESTERN AND EASTERN TSIN, AND THE SOUTHERN AND NORTHERN DYNASTIES
(220 — 589 A.D.)

XXII / Ceramics of the Tsin and Southern and Northern Dynasties from Chekiang, Kiangsu, and Honan Provinces
(265 — 589 A.D.)

236

236. Celadon jar crowned with
miniature buildings and
human figures
Latter half of 3rd century A.D.
(Western Tsin)
Height 46.6 cm.
Unearthed in 1965 at
Shaohsing, Chekiang

237. Celadon vase in shape of an eagle
First half of 4th century A.D. (Western Tsin)
Height 17 cm.
Unearthed in 1964 at Nanking, Kiangsu

238

238. Celadon lion-shaped vessel
Latter half of 3rd century A.D. (Western Tsin)
Length 17.5 cm.
Unearthed in 1966 at Tanyang, Kiangsu

239. Celadon pot ornamented with the head of a cock
       4th century A.D. (Eastern Tsin)
       Height 23.5 cm.
       Unearthed in 1967 at Yuyao, Chekiang

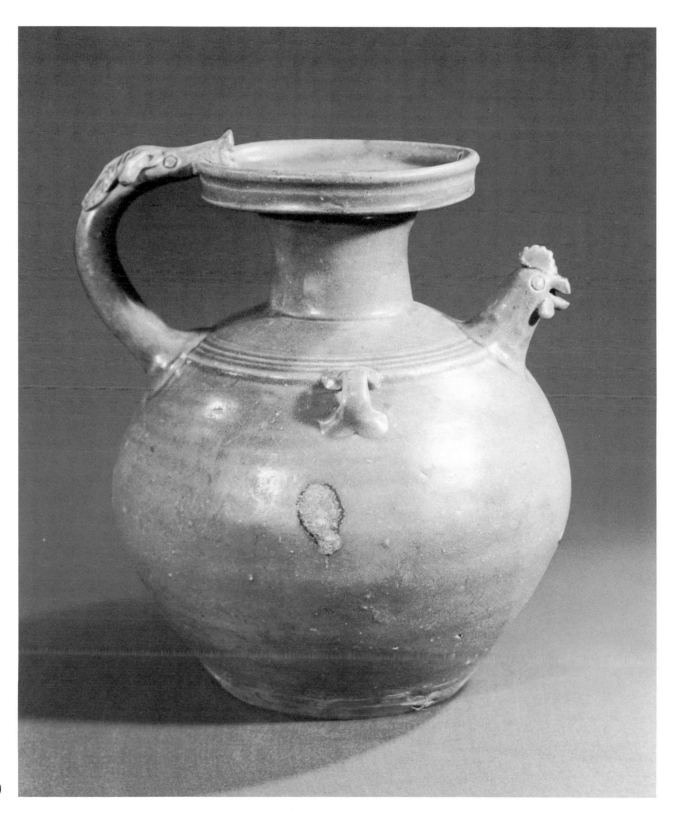

240. Celadon vase with dish mouth and eight rings
First half of 6th century A.D. (Southern Dynasties)
Height 26 cm.
Unearthed in 1964 at Juian, Chekiang

241

241. Celadon jar with incised design
    Latter half of 6th century A.D. (Northern Chi)
    Height 29 cm.
    Unearthed in 1958 at Puyang, Honan

242. Yellowish green-glazed jar with dark green splashes
and four rings
Latter half of 6th century A.D. (Northern Chi)
Height 23.5 cm.
Unearthed in 1958 at Puyang, Honan.

243. Yellow-glazed flat flask decorated with musicians and dancers
Latter half of 6th century A.D. (Northern Chi)
Height 20.5 cm.
Unearthed in 1971 at Anyang, Honan

243

244. Stone carved with dragons and tigers
5th century A. D. (Northern Wei)
Height 16.5 cm., width 32 cm.
Unearthed in 1966 at Tatung, Shansi

245. Stone carved with figures of musicians, dancers, dragons, and tigers
5th century A.D. (Northern Wei)
Height 16.5 cm., width 32.6 cm.
Unearthed in 1966 at Tatung, Shansi

244

245

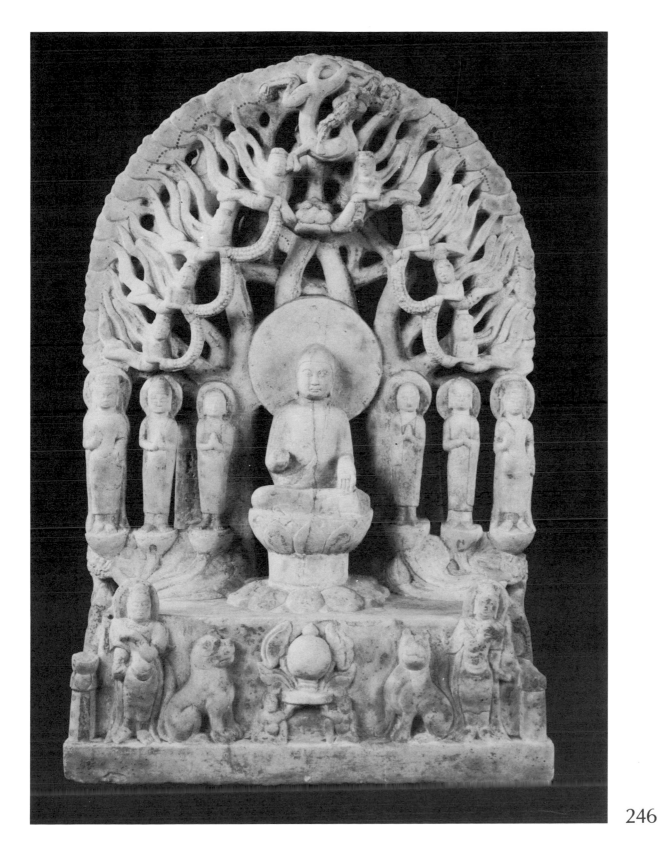

246. Stone image of Sakyamuni in the act of preaching
    Latter half of 6th century A.D. (Northern Chi)
    Height 72.6 cm.
    Unearthed in 1958 at Linchang, Hopei

247. Brocade mitten with the characters:
Yen Nien Yi Shou
1st - 2nd century A.D. (Eastern Han)
Length 24 cm.
Unearthed in 1959 from a site at Niya,
Minfeng county in Sinkiang

248, 249. Two pieces of woolen fabric with
grape pattern
1st - 2nd century A.D. (Eastern Han)
Length 22.5 cm. and 26 cm.
Unearthed in 1959 from site at Niya,
Minfeng county in Sinkiang

248, 249

247

250

250. Woolen girdle
1st - 2nd century A.D. (Eastern Han)
Length 29 cm.
Unearthed in 1959 from a site at Niya, Minfeng
county in Sinkiang

251. Yellow damask with lozenge pattern
1st - 2nd century A.D. (Eastern Han)
Length 24.5 cm.
Unearthed in 1959 from a site at Niya, Minfeng
county in Sinkiang

251

252

252. Brocade with tree pattern
6th century A.D. (Northern Dynasties)
Length 20.5 cm.
Unearthed in 1959 from Astana, Turfan county
in Sinkiang

253. Blue woolen fabric with pattern dyed by the
wax-resist technique (batik)
5th century A.D. (Northern dynasties)
Length 11 cm.
Unearthed in 1959 from Wuyulaike, Yutien
county in Sinkiang

253

254

254. Brocade with flowers-and-birds design
8th century A.D. (Tang dynasty)
Length 38.2 cm.
Unearthed in 1968 from Astana, Turfan county
in Sinkiang

255. Brocade with motif of confronted birds
7th century A.D. (Tang dynasty)
Length 26 cm.
Unearthed in 1969 from Astana, Turfan county
in Sinkiang

255

256. Brocade with picture of a drinking pair
8th century A.D. (Tang dynasty)
Length 12.8 cm.
Unearthed in 1969 from Astana, Turfan county
in Sinkiang

257. Yellow gauze with design of confronted birds, dyed
by the wax-resist technique (batik)
8th century A.D. (Tang dynasty)
Length 57 cm.
Unearthed in 1968 from Astana, Turfan county
in Sinkiang

258. Tang dynasty register of household and land allocation:
household of Ning Ho-tsai, Kaochang County
689 A.D.
29 cm. x 82.3 cm.
Unearthed in 1964 from Astana, Turfan county in Sinkiang

258

259

260

261, 262

263

259. Loan contract signed by Pai Huai-lo as debtor
670 A.D.
29 cm. x 43 cm.
Unearthed in 1964 from Astana, Turfan county in Sinkiang

260. Fried bread-roll
7th century A.D. (Tang dynasty)
Length 18 cm.
Unearthed in 1960 from Astana, Turfan county in Sinkiang

261, 262. Two *chiaotzu* (dumplings)
7th century A.D. (Tang dynasty)
Length 5 cm. and 6 cm.
Unearthed in 1960 from Astana, Turfan county in Sinkiang

263. Silver Sassanian coin
Diameter 2.9 cm.
Unearthed in 1967 from Astana, Turfan county in Sinkiang

SUI DYNASTY
(581 — 618 A.D.)

XXV / Chang Sheng's Tomb of the Sui Dynasty at Anyang, Honan Province
(595 A.D.)

264

264. White porcelain figure of a warrior
Height 64 cm.

265 - 272. Eight painted pottery musicians
Height 17.2 cm. - 19 cm.

273. White porcelain figure of an
attendant, partly in black glaze
Height 71 cm.

273

274. Octagonal gold cup decorated with human figures
Height 5.4 cm., major axis 7 cm., minor axis 6.3 cm.

275. Silver box with bird and flower design
Height 6 cm., dia. 13.5 cm.

274

275

276. Silver bowl with gilt floral design
     Height 3 cm., dia. of mouth 10.1 cm.

277. Silver winged-cup with gilt floral design
     Height 2.8 cm., major axis 10.5 cm.,
     minor axis 8.6 cm.

276

277

278

278. Covered silver bowl with gilt floral design
Height 11.4 cm., dia. of mouth 21.9 cm.

279. Silver *yi* with gilt floral design
Height 8.3 cm.

279

280

280. Gold bowl with embossed lotus-petal design
Height 5.5 cm., dia. of mouth 13.5 cm.

281 - 284. Silver box containing cinnabar and jade
        girdle ornaments
        Height of box 6.2 cm., dia. of mouth 17 cm.

285, 286. Silver box containing stalactite
        Height of box 6.4 cm., dia. of mouth 17 cm.

281 — 284

285, 286

287, 288

289, 290

291, 292

287, 288. Silver plate and cinnabar
  Height of plate 1.9 cm., dia. of
  mouth 14.1 cm.

289, 290. Amber and silver plate
  Height of plate 1.9 cm., dia. of
  mouth 14.3 cm.

291, 292. Rock crystal and silver plate
  Height of plate 1.7 cm., dia. of
  mouth 18.1 cm.

293, 294

295

293, 294. Amethyst and silver plate
Height of plate 1.7 cm., dia. of mouth
18.7 cm.

295. Silver vessel in shape of pomegranate
Height 8.9 cm.

297

296

296. Three-colored pottery horse
Height 28 cm.

297. Yellow-glazed pottery horse
Height 20.1 cm.

298. Three-colored pottery
mounted hunter
Height 32 cm.

298

299. Three-colored pottery mounted hunter
Height 31 cm.

300. Painted pottery horseman
Height 32 cm.

301. Painted pottery horseman
Height 30.5 cm.

300

299

302. Painted pottery
mounted hunter
Height 31.5 cm.

302

303

303. Three-colored pottery bowl
Height 7.4 cm., dia. of mouth
17.2 cm.

304. Three-colored pottery dish
Height 2.7 cm., dia. of mouth
15 cm.

305. Green-glazed pottery bowl
Height 8 cm., dia. of mouth
13.7 cm.

304

305

306

306. Women attendants, wall painting in the
     tomb of Princess Yung Tai (copy)
     192 cm. x 440 cm.

307, 308. Incised figures of palace ladies on the stone
sarcophagus of Princess Yung Tai (rubbings)
136 cm. x 81 cm.

307

308

XXVIII / Fine and Applied Arts of Tang Dynasty
(618 — 907 A.D.)

309. Three-colored pottery horse
Early 8th century A.D.
Height 80 cm., length 82.5 cm.
Unearthed in 1971 from the tomb of Crown Prince Yi Teh
at Chienhsien, Shensi

310, 311. Three-colored pottery pack-camel and groom
8th century A.D.
Height of groom 29.7 cm., height of camel 47.5 cm.,
length 40 cm.
Unearthed in 1959 at Chungpao village, Sian, Shensi

310, 311

312, 313

312, 313. Three-colored pottery horse and groom
8th century A.D.
Height of groom 29 cm., height of horse 40.6 cm.,
length 42.4 cm.
Unearthed in 1959 at Chungpao village, Sian, Shensi

312

314, 315. Three-colored pottery
    figurines of women
    8th century A.D.
    Height 42 cm. and 45 cm.
    Unearthed in 1959 at Chungpao
    village, Sian, Shensi

314

315

316. Three-colored pottery warrior
8th century A.D.
Height 65.5 cm.
Unearthed in 1959 at
Chungpao village, Sian, Shensi

317. Three-colored pottery tomb-
guardian
8th century A.D.
Height 57.5 cm.
Unearthed in 1959 at
Chungpao village, Sian, Shensi

317

318. Yellow-glazed pottery ox in lying position
8th century A.D.
Length 46 cm.
Unearthed in 1965 at Chinan county, Kansu

319. Three-colored phoenix-head vase
8th century A.D.
Height 32.2 cm.
Unearthed in 1961 at Loyang, Honan

318

319

320

320. Covered pot of three-colored pottery
8th century A.D.
Height 21 cm.
Unearthed in 1958 at Loyang, Honan

321. White porcelain spittoon
9th century A.D.
Height 10.5 cm.
Unearthed in 1955 at Sian, Shensi

321

322. High-stemmed porcelain bowl
with applied floral decoration
7th century A.D.
Height 23 cm.
Unearthed in 1956 at Sian, Shensi

323. Celadon vase with applied design in dark brown
    9th century A.D.
    Height 22.5 cm.
    Unearthed in 1958 at Changsha, Hunan

323

324

324. Bronze mirror with hunting design
7th century A.D.
Diameter 29 cm.
Unearthed in 1961 at Fukou, Honan

325

325 Bronze mirror with double-phoenix design
7th century A.D.
Diameter 23 cm.
Unearthed in 1952 at Hsienyang, Shensi

326

326. Bronze mirror with bird and animal design
7th century A.D.
Diameter 21.5 cm.
Unearthed in 1955 at Sian, Shensi

327

328

327, 328. Procession scene,
wall painting in the tomb of
Crown Prince Chang Huai
(2 copies)
Early 8th century A.D.
150 cm. x 240 cm.,
148 cm. x 204 cm.

XXIX / Five Dynasties Tomb at Linan, Chekiang Province, Excavated in 1969
(10th century A.D.)

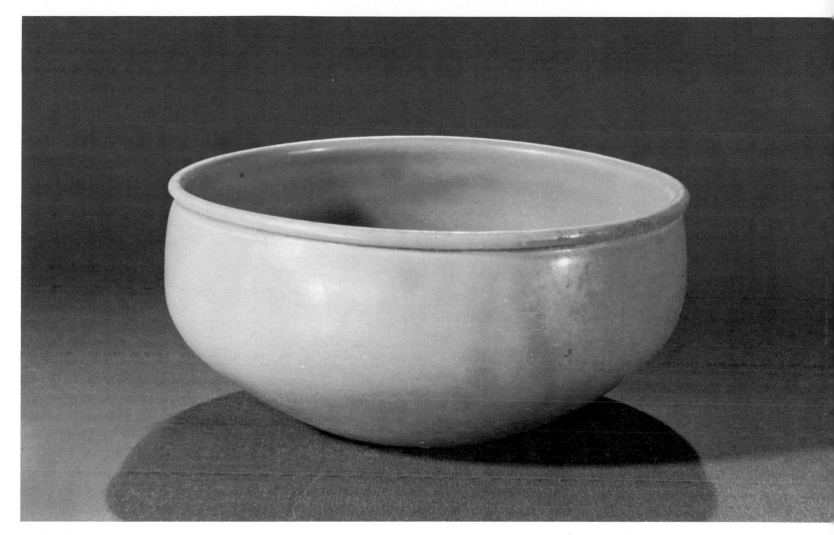

330

329. Porcelain vase with cloud design, Yueh ware
     Height 50.7 cm.

330. Bowl, Yueh ware
     Height 9.5 cm., dia. of mouth 19.9 cm.

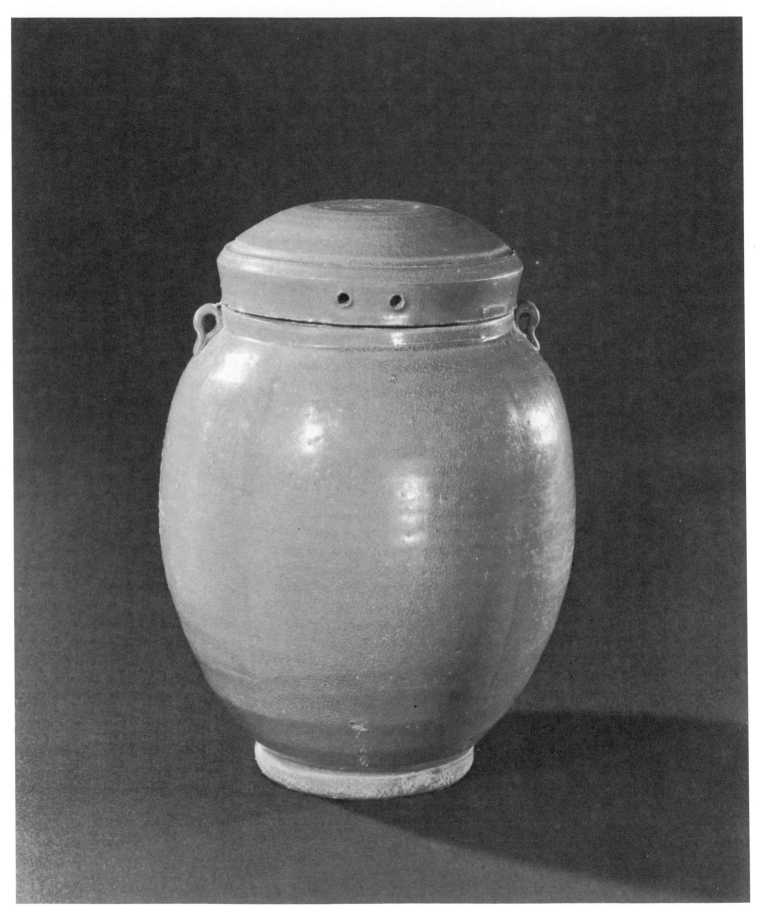

331

331. Two-eared covered jar, Yueh ware
Height 19.6 cm.

332. Two-eared kettle-shaped vessel, Yueh ware
Height 9.2 cm., dia. of mouth 17.6 cm

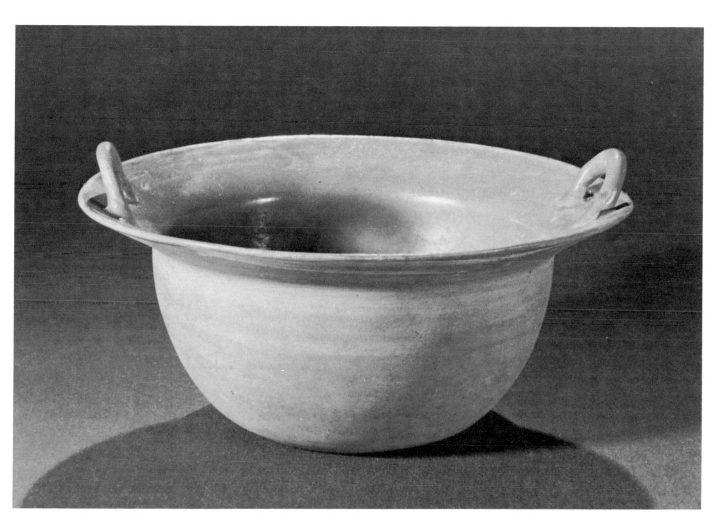

332

XXX / Sung Dynasty Porcelain
(960 — 1279 A.D.)

333

334

333. Bowl with lotus flower design, Ting ware
     10th century A.D.
     Height 7.3 cm., dia. of mouth 21.9 cm.
     Unearthed in 1969 from the foundation of the
     Chingchih Monastery pagoda, Tinghsien
     county, Hopei province

334. Porcelain conch, Ting ware
     10th century A.D.
     Height 19.8 cm.
     Unearthed in 1969 from the foundation of
     the Chingchih Monastery pagoda, Tinghsien
     county, Hopei province

335. Censer with five feet, Ting ware
     10th century A.D.
     Height 24.1 cm.
     Unearthed in 1969 from the foundation of the
     Chingchih Monastery pagoda, Tinghsien
     county, Hopei province

336

336. Flower-shaped dish marked with the
character "kuan", Ting ware
10th century A.D.
Height 3 cm., dia. of mouth 12.8 cm.
Unearthed in 1969 from the foundation of
the Chingchih Monastery pagoda,
Tinghsien county, Hopei province

337. White vase *(kendi)* with
carved decoration, Ting ware
10th century A.D.
Height 60.5 cm.
Unearthed in 1969 from the
foundation of the
Chingchung Monastery
pagoda, Tinghsien county,
Hopei province

338

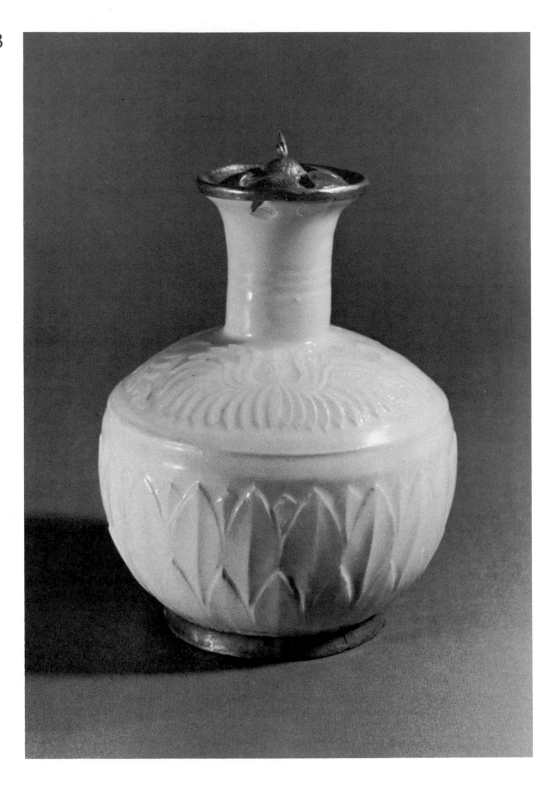

338. Flask incised with floral design, with a silver cover, Ting ware
      10th century A.D.
      Height 19.8 cm.
      Unearthed in 1969 from the foundation of the Chingchung
      Monastery pagoda, Tinghsien county, Hopei province

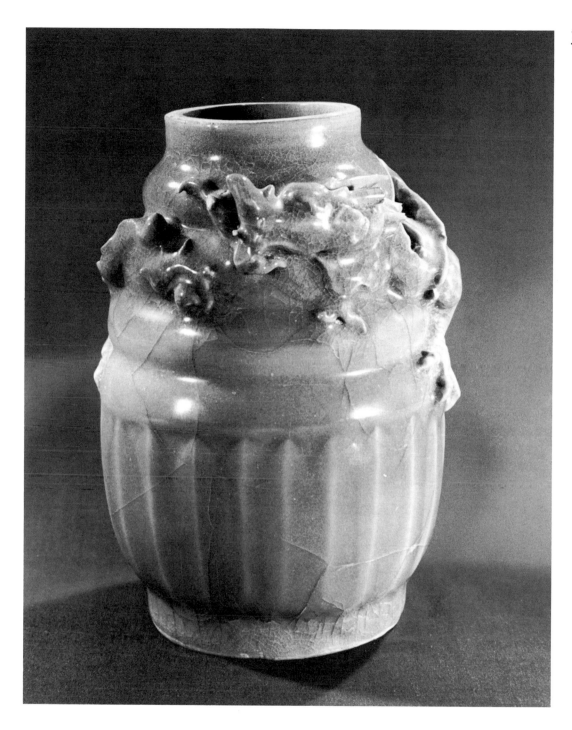

339. Vase decorated with dragon design, Lungchuan ware
12th century A.D.
Height 19 cm.
Unearthed in 1956 at the site of the Great Kiln *(Tayao),*
Lungchuan county, Chekiang

340. Bowl with lotus-petal design, Lungchuan ware
Early 13th century A.D.
Height 6.5 cm., dia. of mouth 13.5 cm.
Unearthed in 1960 at the site of the Great Kiln (Tayao),
Lungchuan county, Chekiang

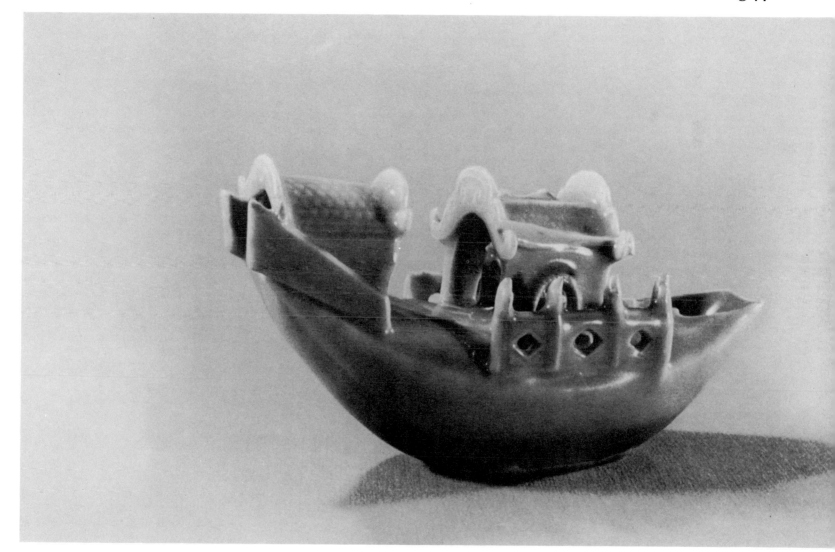

341. Water-dropper in shape of a boat, Lungchuan ware
12th century A.D.
Length 17.3 cm.
Unearthed in 1956 at Lungchuan, Chekiang

342

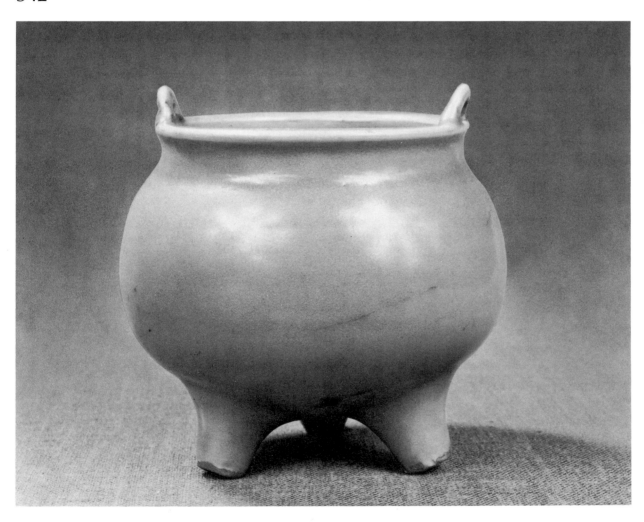

342. Tripod censer, Lungchuan ware
Early 13th century A.D.
Height 12.4 cm.
Unearthed in 1954 at Juian county, Chekiang

343

343. Ying-ching wine pot with warmer
11th century A.D.
Height of pot 25.8 cm., height of warmer 14 cm.
Unearthed in 1963 at Susung, Anhwei

344. Ying-ching bowl
13th century A.D.
Height 9.8 cm.,
dia. 21.2 cm.
Unearthed in 1965 at
Tehan, Kiangsi

345. Ying-ching bowl incised
with floral design
12th century A.D.
Height 7.2 cm., dia. of
mouth 20.5 cm.
Unearthed in 1952 at
Nanchang, Kiangsi

346. Tripod censer, Yaochow ware
13th century A.D.
Height 27 cm.
Unearthed in 1960 at Lantian, Shensi

346

347. Pillow with fishing design, Tzuchow ware
12th century A.D.
Length 28.8 cm.
Unearthed in 1955 at Hsingtai, Hopei

347

遼
金
元

THE LIAO, KIN, AND YUAN DYNASTIES
(916 — 1368 A.D.)

XXXI / Tomb of a Liao Princess's Consort at Chihfeng,
Liaoning Province, Excavated in 1953
(959 A.D.)

349

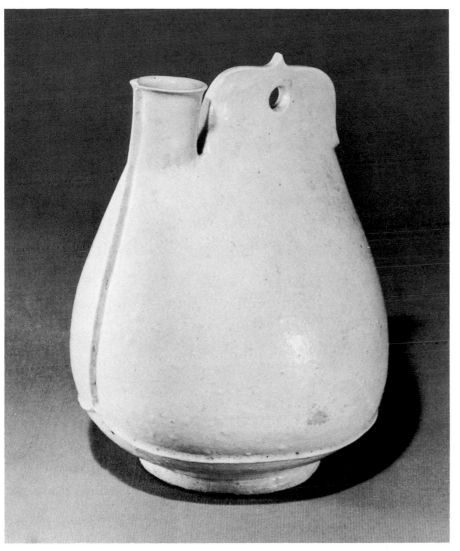

348. White porcelain plate marked with the character "kuan"
Height 5.4 cm., dia. of mouth 22.3 cm.

349. White porcelain flat flask ornamented with cockscomb
Height 23.5 cm.

348

350, 351

350, 351. Two iron heads of
whistling arrows
Length 10 cm. and 9.5 cm.

352, 353. Two gilt silver saddle
ornaments
Height 27.7 cm. and 37.5 cm.

352, 353

354. Silver cup with stand
Height 8.5 cm., dia. of stand 16 cm.

355. Gilt silver tassel ornament for horse
Height 6 cm., dia. 19.2 cm.

354

355

356 — 358

356 - 358. Three pottery actors
13th century A.D. (Kin)
Height 19.5 cm. - 21 cm.
Unearthed in 1965 at Houma, Shansi

359

359. Pottery actor dancing
14th century A.D. (Yuan)
Height 39.2 cm.
Unearthed in 1963 at Chiaotso, Honan

360

360. Pottery actor with clappers
     14th century A.D. (Yuan)
     Height 37 cm.
     Unearthed in 1963 at Chiaotso, Honan

361

361. Pottery actor whistling
     14th century A.D. (Yuan)
     Height 37 cm.
     Unearthed in 1963 at Chiaotso, Honan

362

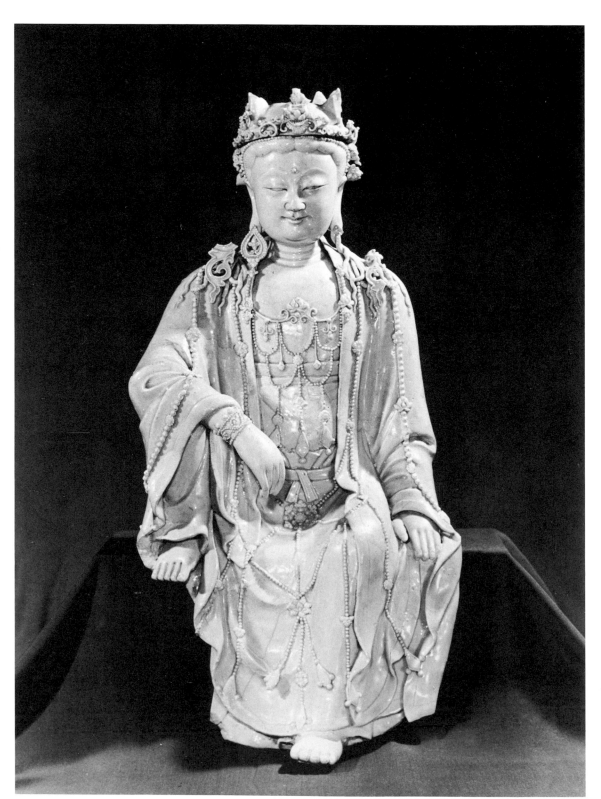

362. Ying-ching statuette
of Kuanyin
1st half of 14th
century A.D.
Height 66 cm.
Unearthed in 1955 in the
west city of Peking

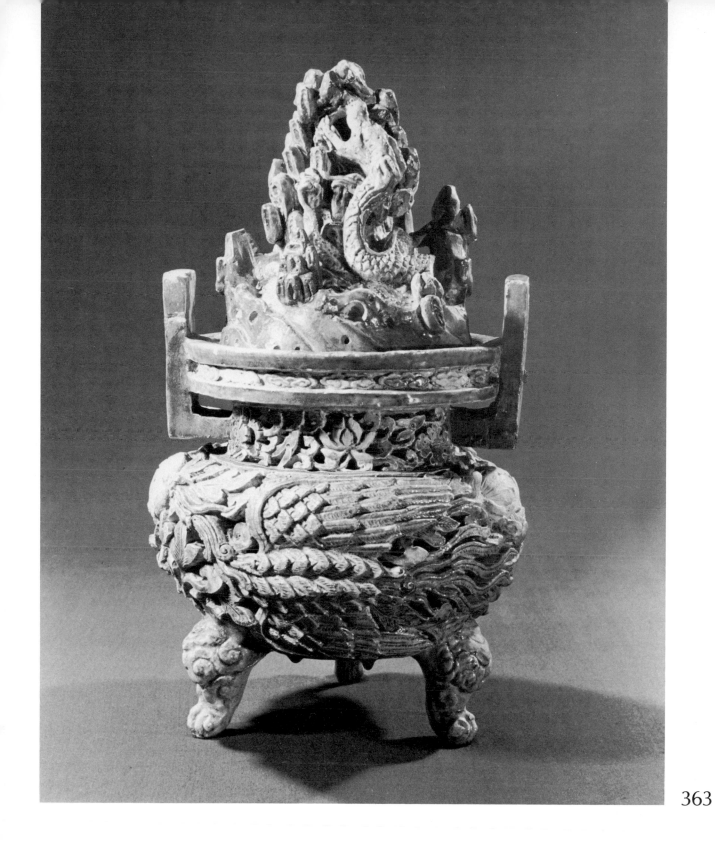

363. Openwork censer of three-colored glazed pottery
End of 13th century A.D.
Height 36 cm.
Unearthed in 1964 in the Haitien district of Peking

364

364. Covered jar with floral
designs in underglaze red
1st half of 14th century A.D.
Height 66 cm.
Unearthed in 1961 in the
Haitien district of Peking

365. Blue-and-white porcelain vase
1st half of 14th century A.D.
Height 15.3 cm.
Unearthed in 1962 in the
west city of Peking

366

366. Plate, Chun ware
1st half of 14th century A.D.
Height 4.5 cm., dia. of mouth 22.3 cm.
Unearthed in 1969 at Fangshan, Peking

367. Ying-ching brush-rest
1st half of 14th century A.D.
Length 18 cm.
Unearthed in 1962 in the west city of Peking

XXXIV / Porcelain, Silver, and Lacquer Wares of the Yuan Dynasty
(1271 — 1368 A.D.)

368. Porcelain jar decorated with two phoenixes in black on white ground
13th century A.D.
Height 36 cm.
Unearthed in 1970 at Fangshan, Peking

369. Blue-and-white covered pot decorated with
white dragon design
1st half of 14th century A.D.
Height 51.5 cm.
Unearthed in 1964 at Paoting, Hopei

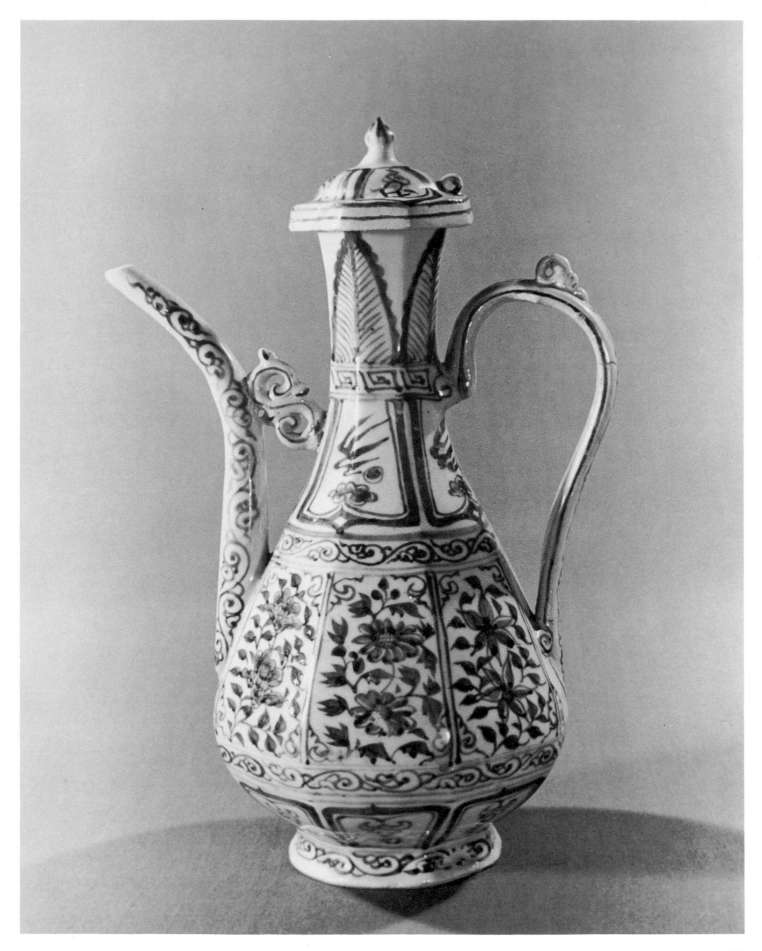

370. Blue-and-white ewer with floral design
1st half of 14th century A.D.
Height 26.5 cm.
Unearthed in 1964 at Paoting, Hopei

371. Basin, Chun ware
13th century A.D.
Height 10.6 cm., dia. of mouth 44 cm.
Unearthed in 1955 at Paoting, Hopei

371

372. Silver confectionery box decorated with
     double-phoenix pattern
     1st half of 14th century A.D.
     15.9 cm., dia. 35 cm.
     Unearthed in 1955 at Hofei, Anhwei

373. Round box of lacquerware carved with human figures
1st half of 14th century A.D.
Height 3.9 cm., dia. 12.1 cm.
Unearthed in 1953 at Chingpu, Shanghai

373

374 - 385. Toilet articles and silver toilet box with stand (12 pieces)
14th century A.D.
Height of box 24.3 cm., dia. 17 cm., height of
mirror-stand 30.4 cm.
Unearthed in 1964 at Soochow, Kiangsu

NOTES

NOTES